TABLE OF CONTENTS

Cuddly Koalas

Koalas grow up in the **wild**.

Baby koalas are called joeys.

How Baby Koalas Look

A newborn joey is the size of a jelly bean. It is **blind** and hairless.

A joey stays in its mother's **pouch**.

It grows bigger.

Joeys grow soft, gray fur. They have patches of white fur.

Joeys have strong arms. They have **claws** on each paw.

How Baby Koalas Sound

Baby koalas make sounds to **communicate**.

They **bellow** to their mothers.

They snarl when they feel scared.

What Baby Koalas Eat

A joey drinks milk inside its mother's pouch. It drinks milk for about six months.

Koalas are **herbivores**. They eat plants. They like **eucalyptus** leaves.

Mothers teach joeys to eat leaves.

They chew up leaves to make **pap**.

Joeys eat the pap.

Lots to Learn

A joey gets too big to fit in the pouch. It comes out to explore. It rides on its mother's back.

Joeys practice climbing trees. They learn which leaves are good to eat.

Joeys must learn to protect themselves in the wild.

All Grown Up

A koala is **mature** when it is about one year old. It leaves its mother. It finds a new home.

Glossary

bellow (BEL-oh): to make a loud, deep sound

blind (blinde): unable to see

claws (klawz): sharp, curved nails on the feet of animals

communicate (kuh-MYOO-ni-kate): to share information and feelings

eucalyptus (yoo-kuh-LIP-tuhs): an evergreen tree that grows in Australia

herbivores (HUR-buh-vorz): animals that eat only plants

mature (muh-CHOOR): fully grown or developed; adult

pap (pap): a soft, partly digested food made by mother koalas for their babies

pouch (pouch): a pocket in the mother's body in which koalas, kangaroos, and other marsupials carry their babies

wild (wilde): natural places where no people live

Thinking Questions

1. What are baby koalas called?
2. What color is a baby koala's fur?
3. How do koala mothers help their babies?
4. What kind of leaves do koalas like to eat?
5. What sounds do baby koalas make?

Index

About the Author

Madison Parker spent her childhood in the city of Chicago, Illinois. A farm girl at heart, today she lives in Wisconsin with her husband and four children on a small farm with cows, goats, chickens, and two miniature horses named Harley and David. Her favorite dessert is vanilla frozen custard with rainbow sprinkles, even in the winter.